Contemporary Turkish
Women Poets

Contemporary Turkish Women Poets

———

Introduced by
SALİHA PAKER

Translated & Edited by
GEORGE MESSO

R·H·B

First published in the United Kingdom in 2009 by Conversation Paperpress.
This edition published 2015 by Red Hand Books

RED HAND BOOKS
Old Bath Road, London SL3 0NS
1618 Yishan Road, Minhang District, 201103 Shanghai
150th Avenue, Springfield Gardens, 11413 New York
Şerifali Mahallesi, Umraniye 34775 Istanbul
Cross Road A, Andheri, 400093 Mumbai

www.rhbks.com

ISBN: 978-1-910346-06-8 (Paperback)

Acknowledgements

The translator and publishers gratefully acknowledge permission to include in this book copyright material, as follows:

Yapı Kredi Yayınları, Istanbul, for poems by Gülten Akın from *Toplu Şiirler II*, 2000, *Kırmızı Karanfil 1956-1971*, 2008, and *Uzak Bir Kıyıda 1984-2003*, 2008; Can Yayınları, Istanbul, for poems by Melisa Gürpınar from *Ada Şiirleri*, 2003; Evrensel Basım Yayın, Istanbul, for poems by Sennur Sezer from *Kirlenmiş Kâğıtlar*, 2009; Komşu Yayınları/Yasakmeyve, Istanbul, for poems by Gülseli İnal from *Toplu Şiirler IV*, 2009; Adam Yayınları, Istanbul, for poems by İnci Asena from *Tramvay Döşeriz Ay Döşeriz*, 1993, and *Çıplak Bakamıyorum*, 1996; Yapı Kredi Yayınları, Istanbul, for poems by Oya Uysal from *Kimselerin Akşamı*, 2007; Yapı Kredi Yayınları, Istanbul, for poems by Lâle Müldür from *Anemon: Toplu Şiirler (1988-1998)*, 2002; Everest Yayınları, Istanbul, for poems by Nilgün Marmara from *Daktiloya Çekilmiş Şiirler*, 2006; Everest Yayınları, Istanbul, for poems by Perihan Mağden from *Dünya İşleri*, 2001; Yapı Kredi Yayınları, Istanbul, for poems by Çiğdem Sezer from *Denizden Geçme Hâli*, 2009; Dünya Yayıncılık, Istanbul, for poems by Zeynep Uzunbay from *Yara Falı*, 2006, and to the poet for poems from a manuscript-in-progress, 2009; Can Yayınları, Istanbul, for poems by Betül Tarıman from *Güle Gece Yorumları*, 2002, and *Yol İnsanları*, 2004; Metis Yayınları, Istanbul, for poems by Bejan Matur from *Rüzgâr Dolu Konaklar*, 1999, *Tanrı Görmesin Harflerimi*, 1999, *Ayın Büyüttüğü Oğullar*, 2002, and *Onun Çölünde*, 2002; İnkılâp Kitabevi, Istanbul, for poems by Didem Madak from *Grapon Kağıtları*; Everest Yayınları, Istanbul, for poems by Zeynep Köylü from *İlk Ağacı Öperek*, 2000; Yapı Kredi Yayınları, Istanbul, for poems by Gonca Özmen from *Belki Sessiz*, 2008, and to the poet for poems from the manuscript of *Kuytumda*, Hera Yayınları, 2000.

Every effort has been made to secure permissions; copyright holders who have not been acknowledged above are invited to contact the publishers forthwith.

A special note of thanks to Semra Şenol, Dr. Şenol Bezci, Professor Saliha Paker, and Gonca Özmen for their support, encouragement and help in seeing this long work to completion.

The translator would also like to thank Translation House, Looren, Switzerland, for a generous residency in the summer of 2009.

Contemporary Turkish Women Poets

CONTENTS

Introduction

Introduction

In Sennur Sezer's "documentary narrative"[1] *Mihrî Hatun, a Turkish Sappho* the author reconstructs the life and times of Mihrî (c.1460–1506), an Ottoman woman who achieved unusual recognition as a poet in the late fifteenth century, but who was only brought to the modern reader's attention within the last few decades.[2]

In *The Age of Beloveds: Love and the Beloved in Early-Modern Ottoman and European Culture and Society* (2005) Walter Andrews and Mehmet Kalpaklı too discuss Mihrî, focusing on "the problem that the woman poet presents for both Hafezan (Persianate) and Petrarchan poetry" - forms almost entirely dominated by men. Offering invaluable insight not only into the gender politics of poetry of the sixteenth century but also of our very 'modern' times, they write:

> The beloved's power is always what the early-modern (/male) poet perceives as feminine - no matter what the beloved's actual gender. That power lies in withholding, denying, inaccessibility, veiling, spirituality, silence, modesty. The beloved acts, if at all, only in the most subtle and ambiguous gestures - the shy glance, timid coquetry. Active love is the masculine role. It is passionate, suffers publicly, speaks aloud. It reveals the beloved and creates the beloved's image by tearing away veils of modesty with gusts of description, making the beloved present to the gaze of the world. Thus, unless the object of her passion is God and, by

---

1 Sezer, Sennur (1997) *Türk Safosu Mihrî Hatun*. Belgesel Anlatı. İstanbul: Milliyet Yayınları.
2 Toska, Zehra (2007) 'Divan şiirinde kadın şairlerin sesi' in Halman, Talat Sait et al (eds.) *Türk Edebiyatı Tarihi*, Vol. 2, Istanbul: T.C. Kültür ve Turizm Bakanlığı Yayınları. - Toska names fifteen women, from the fifteenth to mid-nineteenth century, only six of whom are represented by their collections of poetry, the earliest one being Mihrî Hatun. Five more, all born in the second half of the nineteenth century, are cited by Bekiroğlu, Nazan (1999) 'Osmanlıda Kadın Şairler' in Güler Eren (ed.) *Osmanlı*. Ankara: Yeni Türkiye Yayınları, Vol. 9.

extension, her own (holy) virtue, the woman poet is taking a man's part and leaving the male poet in a quandary. Either becoming a poet is the same as abandoning the (supposedly) female virtues, or presumed gender distinctions and categories no longer hold.[3]

Sennur Sezen's biography brings up this subject of "honour" or "untouchedness." She notes that the Ottoman biographers defended Mihrî Hatun's "innocence", "chastity and celibacy", how Mihrî herself was careful to protect her reputation in the provincial town of Amasya where she lived; that, for instance, the poem where she prayed to God "not to reveal her secrets, lest they stoned down her home" was omitted from her collection presented to the Sultan (Bayezid II) and predictably, her more passionate poems were also excluded from the main manuscripts of her work while others were toned down or more heavily veiled. Having pointed out that it was "foreign" scholars who described Mihrî as a 'Turkish Sappho' with reference to her poetic gifts and private life, Sezer writes that in view of punishments that she might be subjected to "Mihrî felt shame and was fearful. Therefore, her (male) contemporaries and later biographers were right in defending her (honour), as they would have done even today. As for me," continues Sezer, "I too find it right not to interfere with the ambiguities about her but to go by the tradition regarding her life and work." [4]

Sennur Sezer's seemingly conservative approach is nevertheless subverted by Mihrî's own poetry which dominates the elegantly reconstructed life. It's through Mihrî's poetry (selected, quoted in the original classical Ottoman and translated into modern Turkish for the contemporary reader) that we discover she dreaded marriage even as a young girl, became a headstrong woman pursuing love but with a genuine ambition to be recognized by the male literary *élite* of her time, including the Sultan himself.

Another poet, Nigâr Hanım (1862-1918) was from an aristocratic

---

3 Andrews, Walter and Kalpaklı, Mehmet (2005) *The Age of Beloveds: Love and the Beloved in Early-Modern Ottoman and European Culture and Society.* London: Duke University Press. p.198.
4 Sezer (1997) p. 128.

family and famous for mixing with men and women in her own literary salon in the late nineteenth century. She wrote in the tradition of court poetry, like the women preceding her, but her individuality found much more vivid expression in the period of acculturation when the Ottomans were becoming more intimately acquainted with European literature and thinking. In stark contrast, there was Yaşar Nezihe (1880-1971), now identified as the Ottoman "woman poet of the proletariat". The literary establishment knew little about her but she was included in a German anthology of "new Turkish poets"[5] . Born to a poor family, Yaşar Nezihe had to make her own living, and became a member of the Workers' Association. At the same time, she wrote for women's magazines and published poems about her own hardships and those of fellow workers – celebrating, for instance, the "First of May", for which she was prosecuted.

Generally speaking, women born to aristocratic or well-to-do families, and able to study Persian (and later, French) and the arts, could gain recognition for their poetry within the established (male) literary circles, tending eventually however to be singled out as "women" poets, and never major ones. Today they are considered part of the historical canon of Turkish poetry thanks to modern scholarship that is motivated by an expanding interest in women's literary studies. Nevertheless, one often detects a note of disappointment in scholarly analyses that do not seem to point to a "distinctively articulated woman's voice" emerging from Ottoman poetry that was by tradition dependent on the convention of classically intricate metaphors and conceits developed and propagated by the male majority.

Perhaps the question is: who set(s) the condition for a "distinctively articulated woman's voice" to be heard in poetry written by women? Bejan Matur seems to sum up the reaction to such an expectation: "Womanhood is in my poetry because I'm a woman, not because I write woman's poetry."[6] Women, not only as poets but as writers of fiction would likely tend to agree with Bejan Matur. If we put aside

---

5 Hartmann, Martin (1919) *Dichter Der Neuen Türkei.* Berlin.
6 Arlı, Sıla (2003) "A Meeting of 'Poet (who are?) Women,' Overshadowed by War," *Bilkent Kanat Dergisi* No.12. Bahar.

popular fiction by women, and the work of Halide Edip, a major novelist of the early twentieth century, we observe that only after the 1960s did women begin to consider writing fiction seriously, which is more or less the time when they also started showing serious interest in writing poetry for publication. The only difference is that many fewer women seem to have "dared" to express themselves publicly as poets than as novelists and short story writers. The novel was a newly attempted genre, going only as far back as the second half of the nineteenth century, while the tradition of poetry could be traced back more than five hundred years. Thanks to poets like Yahya Kemal (1884-1958), poetic continuity seems to have suffered less from the civilizational rupture with the Ottomans, which resulted from the republican reforms of the late 1920s and 30s. Because of the change in the alphabet in 1928 (from Arabic to Roman letters, to facilitate and enhance literacy), women and men born in the 1930s could not read or understand earlier poetry in its original form. This meant that often they lost touch with whatever earlier poetry had been written by their foremothers, except that which existed in the oral tradition and folklore; in anonymous songs and dirges.

To paraphrase Zeynep Uzunbay,[7] men speak in their poetry of and for women all the time, so perhaps they need to hear the new "voices" that they themselves cannot or will not produce. Perhaps they want to hear something outstanding, challenging or even outrageous? They seem to forget, however, that women grew up as poets reading poetry written by men: Tevfik Fikret (1867-1915), Ahmet Haşim (1884-1933), Yahya Kemal (1884-1958), and Nazım Hikmet (1902-1963) the "Strange Poetry" of Orhan Veli, Oktay Rifat and Melih Cevdet, and the "Second New."

A younger generation of women would also have read Gülten Akın[8], the first woman to achieve unequivocal recognition and prominence in the literary establishment. Back in the 1980s, Memet Fuat, stepson of Nazım Hikmet and a highly influential critic and editor, included Gülten Akın as the only woman among the 82

---

7 In a personal communication.

8 Sürsal, Hilal (2008) *Voice of Hope: Turkish Woman Poet Gulten Akin.* Indiana University Press.

poets in his anthology (1985)[9]. In his preface he introduced Akın, pointing out that initially her poetry was finely accentuated by "individual emotions": this must have been the time when Gülten "cut her black, black hair"[10], making her instantly popular. But in Memet Fuat's view she was "not in the vanguard" until "she suddenly made a breakthrough in the 1970s, turning towards social issues, reflecting the suffering brought about by conflicts in the country. She wrote with a modern perception of the traditional elements of the Anatolian popular epic, elegy and song, and spoke out for resistance to brute force and repression. She reflected the constructive anger of woman's sensitivity, and of motherhood." [11] Apart from revealing a certain attitude, these words describe Gülten Akın's elegies well, especially her *Poems of 42 Days* [12], first published in 1986. This is a powerful collection that focuses on the mothers of young political prisoners on a hunger strike as violence ran rife, and it marks the painful consequences of the occurrence of no less than three military coups in three decades (1960, 1971, 1980). The final one has left a bitter legacy which the present political system has yet to eradicate.

In this volume, Melisa Gürpınar's lyrical, private world, celebrating ordinary life in Istanbul, and Sennur Sezer's blend of individual and social(ist) conscience, follow the selection from Gülten Akın. It is worth noting that both Gürpınar and Sezer had each published five collections by 1985, when Memet Fuat brought out his anthology, but nevertheless they were left out. Fifteen years later, along with twenty other women, they were represented in Yılmaz Odabaşı's popular anthology, *Anthology of Poetry of the Last Quarter-Century: 1975-2000*, which covers the work of 195 poets, born from the 1940s onwards. This, of course, indicates not just the growing numbers but a quite striking rise as well in the number of women who were

---

9 Fuet, Memet (1985).

10 Messo, George (ed.) (2007) "I Cut My Black, Black Hair," *Near East Review*. Trans. Paker, Saliha & Kenne, Mel.

11 Fuat, Memet quoted in Paker, Saliha (1991) 'Unmuffled Voices in the Shade and Beyond: Women's Writing in Turkish' in Scott, Helena Frsas, (ed.) *Textual Liberation: European Feminist Writing in the Twentieth Century*. New York: Routledge.

12 A translation of Akın, Gülten (1986) *Poems of 42 Days* is in preparation. Trans. Paker, Saliha & Kenne, Mel, to be published by Talisman House (New Jersey).

committed to writing and publishing their poetry. The present volume covers most of those names as well as a few more, including Gonca Özmen, born in 1982.

Some of these poets have been and are now involved in criticism and reviewing, critical and political journalism[13], fiction and essay writing, and publishing. One poet who has devoted herself entirely to her work, winning outstanding critical acclaim among a younger generation of poets writing in Turkey, is Birhan Keskin, whose writing has been described by Hüseyin Ferhad "as a testament in itself to the language of Turkish poetry after the 1980s."[14] Could these words also be taken as the forging of a new poetics beyond the gender divide?

In an interview given on the launch of her new book *Soğuk Kazı* (*Cold Dig*) in 2010, Keskin notes: "the poet's problem is integrated with life, and moves along with life, like that of the poor. We can also describe it as climbing up a hill with never a break and a sack-full of hard, hurting chestnuts on your back."[15] Isn't "life" here, integral with the "poet's problem", regardless of gender?

When poets speak in interviews and on other occasions, they generally highlight struggle, conflicts personal and political, and, of course, resistance. We still hear calls for women to be "brave and courageous" in matters relating to poetry and literature in general, despite a certain contemporary women's discourse that tones down gender discrimination, reflecting the view that things have changed since their childhood. Sennur Sezer points out that she had stayed away from poetry for a long time because early in her career being designated as a "woman poet" was felt to be contemptible. However, Didem Madak, younger than Sezer, claims that cultural codes set down by men continue to push women out, and that women still

---

13 Perihan Mağden is equally well known as columnist and novelist; her fiction has been translated into many languages including English. Ece Temelkuran (not in this volume) has made a name for herself primarily as a newspaper columnist and journalist but has also recently published a novel. It must also be said that Bejan Matur's work in poetry has not been overshadowed by her quite recent involvement in journalism. Her second book of poems in English translation (Trans. Christie, Ruth) is forthcoming from Arc, UK.
14 Özmen, Gonca (2010) 'Çorak dünyamızda 'Soğuk Kazı'' *Radikal Kitap*, 9 April.
15 *ibid.*

need to be encouraged. Emphasis differs of course from poet to poet. For Gülseli İnal, for instance, poetry is about building a new relationship with the world, bringing down boundaries, doing away with brutality, and calling for peace and love. Bejan Matur stresses "poets' addiction to language,"[16] regardless of gender.

Each poet finds, in her own way, the means to weave these concerns into her poetics, through metaphors which, though they may start with "home, mother, father, child, husband and lover," extend beyond them, into the politics of love, secret or otherwise, the politics of repression, crises of confidence, social frustration, personal anxiety, disgust and protest, mysticism, fantasy, and attempts to come to terms with historical injustice. What finally emerges is each of these women's tremendous confidence in their own power of expression.

Each poem, as always, speaks for itself. In this volume it is the selection and sequencing of the poems and their translations that reveal the individual voice of every poet, while the anthology as a whole speaks for "contemporary Turkish women poets". Translation builds a metaphorical bridge so that English-speaking readers may cross over to the original language of each poet's work, into some of the most fertile yet least-known terrain of modern Turkish literature. That this terrain finds life, song, and 'survival' in English by a *man* – a poet, translator and anthologist – brings an aesthetic dimension of its own to this book: the first of its kind in English.

Saliha Paker

---

16 Sıla (2003).

Gülten Akın

Gülten Akın is one of Turkish poetry's most pioneering and distinguished voices. Born in Yozgat in 1933, she studied at Ankara College for Girls and later graduated from Ankara University's Faculty of Law. Her first poems appeared in 1951 and she has since gone on to win almost every major poetry award in Turkey, including the prestigious Golden Orange Poetry Prize, in 1999, and, more recently, the Erdal Öz Literature Prize, in 2008.

Yellow Crocus on a Wire

I saw them on mountains I saw them on roads
A fox's son a fox was climbing a hill
Cats all day in the trees
What's the connection between wind and a tortoise
Pigs stretch out against the day
A rhinoceros at the head of a slope

Prison guard prison guard
The foals are bound
Gazelles are in fetters

A yellow crocus
Suddenly blocking my way on a hill
If I take them to their dorms
If I take them away I can't
My hands on the wire

A desolate yellow crocus
A cool little crocus on a wire
My beloved on the other side
His body half light half shade
Through concrete courts and walls
Daylight thumps into my eyes my eyes
Sometimes he sees me sometimes I see him
I hear his voice his voice his voice
I put it behind me
Overcome it through spring floods
Pass beyond through pathless mountains

Prison guard prison guard
This vacillating world
This ever deathly world
Your strength is the mirror of my weakness
Autumn sun glittering in water

I do not sigh because I know
What nights bring in their wake
Resolve my tangled mess you think unsolved
Fetters crumbling into dust

I do not sigh
My beloved does not sigh

Stain

We stood at the filthiest place of our age
Someone should write us, if not ourselves
Then who
The knife we used to whittle rough days
Got blunter the quieter it became
Where are they, in all that stirs?
The flashing miracle, the sparkling magic
One more day unseen
One more day passed, wilting the grass

We learnt it was blind, as if non-existent
Neither road nor passerby
Nor anyone to note who came and went
They said
Lock them up, leave the key in its former place
And yet
It's a shameful thing, says Camus
To be happy alone
Voices and other voices, where are the world's voices
The stain penetrates the tissue
Silently, becoming silent

Gülten Akın

Ballad of a Working Mother's Child

I tossed them out. What use are paints
For loneliness except for black
What colour can I use
Dry table, dim ceiling, sulking carpet
My picture should be pale

My window draws no birds
The daffodils lost their breath
With three brushes you couldn't comb Yuku-Lili's hair
I'm the child of a working mother

On roads, on roofs snow falls and mutes
The blue lines left from summer past
I'm quiet. Joy's sounds also
Trying once or twice fall silent
Cat-calls at the foot of a wall
In gardens ugly chrysanthemums should be opening

Wedding and Snow

The warm glow of a wedding's sadness
Matched by dense snow and the desolate night
They passed us in a doorway
Only the little girl, the young woman
The rest left inside
Just the two of us in the whole street

Snow on my chest, up to your knees
With your white mohair scarf
We walked
The rest left there
Estranged somehow or else bound
To those winter pleasures and warm rooms

Snow mounted up and our feet
Were too heavy for our thin bodies
We were freezing
As we trudged uphill
Where we stopped at the swing-door
Embraced, and wept

So motionless, so soft
Their sad smiles
Of thin silk
Crazy yet hesitant
Uniting the furthest threads
Standing there with such pride

Your death just a breath away
An insurmountable wall rose up
In the snow of those nights to follow
Alone with the pain, spellbound,
Stung with longing,
I walked on

Surly Gypsy

I'm the silver fox of an epic hunt
I ran the length of rivers, ran in snow
I gave up, couldn't kill, life was precious
I turned and hunted myself

The lines were ready, giving life to whoever wanted it
Ready, I made of it a fairy tale

I'm the sun's surly gypsy, I tracked the sun
Roads bled with longing, mountains echoed my name
I became a tree my fruit shaken off, I was satisfied
My feet walked within me

I am Hallac, I am Nesimi, so much did I believe
That I left my skin

I held death death
Renounced from afar
Like a screw from its own silence
It got used to me

Dilemma

The most valuable thing life gifted me
The thorny necklace of a sheep dog
Sometimes I'm an empty seashell on a beach
Sometimes I'm a sea that cannot reach its shore
I steadied myself with backwards steps
I love life and I love you.

My Barbed-Wire Self

Cheat me fool me
Let them stay like that
Realities pulled from under me
Let savagery freeze

Were it even a faded flower
It's my life my life
Let it stay like my life

Return? I don't want return
Let the past stay put
Let it stay like that, save the day
Save me save me
Save me myself

Geranium

Let's recall, it's a law:
No one can halt the rain
Of those who stitch seeds, plan seedlings,
No one can block their sun

I'm stitching basil, planting geraniums
Vigorous, so my neighbour says
Now, if you like it or not,
Seeds will open, spread out across your earth

Wonderful wonderful wonderful my god
I'm stitching basil, planting geraniums
I'm spurring the vigour of flower and herb
From this day forth vigour
Will mean resistance and hope
To be inseparably intimate
And identical with life
Believe me friends, believe me
The geranium snapped from its stalk
Never wilted once, never bent its head
Opening now where I planted it

Caretaker Women Poem

Lowering their voices, reducing words
Bowing their heads
Slowly they emerge from underground

In purple scarves and orange sweaters
Caretaker women, husbands, kids
Transform our waste cities into gardens
Pale then paler then paler still
Their faces fly as far as night

Sand

I had a lover
Who sent sand from the city where he lived
And yet it was the wind there I always wondered about
Was it tame wild incessant?
Did it suddenly appear hurling in the sky
What it took from the ground?

Later there were cities we shared
The wind a master but me untrained
It blew, raging, came and went
Sand filled my eyes

Melisa Gürpınar

Melisa Gürpınar was born in Istanbul in 1941. After graduating from the Theatre department of Istanbul State Conservatory she studied in London, where she also worked for the Turkish broadcasting section of the BBC World Service. She has won many awards and has been a prominent member of the Turkish Writer's Association and Turkish PEN.

from Island Poems

2

Though it's called
A desert island,
Formed by
A violent quake,
There isn't so much
As a dot on the map.
It's clearly

Outside all geographies,
No compass
Shows its direction.
Its journey
Follows no ship's course.
Alone
Beneath a rainbow,
Forgetting night and day
And the unrelenting noise
Of the universe,
Sleeping in fog
Innocently like a small child.
And on its naked neck
There must be a necklace
Made of sand
Carried back and forth
By waves each season.

No traveler
Has yet reached
So dark a place as this.
Those who wrote
The history of solitude
Call it the sea's heart.
Perhaps it was a monster
Spewing fire,
Which cooled with time
And fused in the bosom of the sea.

But this is hearsay,
Only poets
Believe in
An island like that.
And after every storm,
They would hear

The island calling them
From afar
Syllable by syllable.

3

Who knows for how many thousand-
Years it's been the scream of writing.
Words that wake with sun
As though wanting to pay life's debt,
With the hurrying dew drop
Tumbling head over heals in the wake
Of a crazy river, rushing head-long to the sea.

Like the old woman sweeping village roads,
Who squeezes a cigarette between purplish lips
Resembling over-ripe cherries,
How is it she no longer counts
The greetings she bids the daylight
And the incessant wave
She gives to travelers
As if she no longer sees them,
Lava mixing with tidal streams,
With the same absent mindedness
Everyone should scrutinize
Their own faces for marks
Of those happier times
Which pass and stop
And then rewind.

Well now soulbirds' wings
Are turning red,
Clouds racing over the sky
Have no power to stop it.

Just as a full-stop at the end of a sentence
Finds its place
And scours its environment,
Waves will also one day
Cloak that distant island .
The old woman in her place
Squats down.
The trellis falls in,
And Chinese roses close up with a bang.
After all
Storm's other name is death,
Round and around it comes
Breaking down the doors
Of our breasts.

4

O woman why do you cry,
Crying for years
With the silence
Of a galleon
In the cold sea of forgetfulness.

That it's you
Was clear
When you first
Met yourself,
That humpbacked solitude
In awe of night
Became brave and reckless
Like a white whale
Chasing moonlight
Over oceans.
They say
Every island

Has two spirits,
One riding the horse of captivity
The other freedom,
Every day with foaming mouths
They compete with waves.
And then
She'll present
A poisonous eye-catching
Poem
To you
From between those slippery rocks.

O woman why do you cry?
With half of your face
Like an unborn child,
The other like a marble altar
Washed by eternity,
When not even
A salt mark will remain
Of your steaming tears.
And the angel of death
Rowing from afar
Will not understand
A word you wrote
With blue ink
On water.

5

Even if I look
I can't find those days,
Those olden days caught
Between wracks of whelks.
Not even a footprint on the beach.
Nothing returns now

So why should the winds of times past?
It's clear they slipped away
Never violating the calm sea
Like shadows of gulls
Flying in the wake of a ferry boat.

What were they I fled from,
Which island was it,
Shelter of my crazed soul?
I think that hidden valley
Stayed locked in my dream-book.
Now those winged angels have aged,
Caught up among finely knitted screens.
In the sky there should've been a paper moon
Full of holes,
And outside my home
A plant heavy with seed,
A wild pear tree
Blond haired infants
And a harmonica too
Which everyone has wanted to play
At least once in their lifetime.

It's as if
On every page of memories
There was some eye-catching trap.
I don't know, how
Was I to escape
The doubts playing over my tongue,
And from the hopeless running
In an empty room
As if hosting a guest
Between the four walls of words?

I became destitute

Never taking off these blind feelings
Winter or summer like a woolen vest,
Sitting on moss-covered stairs
Smiling into emptiness,
Never knowing who it is
That comes and goes.

Sennur Sezer

Sennur Sezer was born in 1943 in Eskişehir. A poet, as well as a prolific essayist and short story writer, Sezer was the 2009 recipient of the Ş. Avni Ölez Poetry Prize. Her many honours also include the 1998 Literature Prize from the Pir Sultan Abdal Society.

Ballad Of A Woman Who Waits

I don't want sadness and worry to cover my face
I've locked up mirrors
Erased hopelessness

Innocent bodies warm dreams of love
One who knows love protects the untouchable
I locked up my nakedness at nights

And whatever there was to lock away
I set it free
Let my thoughts fuse with yours
I'll taste what you've seen

Don't let our different lives come between us
Not even in dreams

I never changed the imprint of your face on the pillow
Your shirts were ironed
I washed everything soiled by the sound of sirens

To wait is the very name of joy
To know that you lived
I will be young again when you return
Don't cover your face with worry

The New Bremen Harmonica Players

Why does the streetlamp lighting wet asphalt
Bring to mind a far off city
Gothic cities
Weighed down by winter and foreignness
And hotel rooms
Growing narrower in the middle of the night

A language that cracks like a whip
A thousand assorted things
And festive lights that estrange you
- Am I so far away from my home
If I fall will someone pick me up
Or will they first ask my identity –
Cold droplets on your brow
And the calling card getting wet in your hand

You seek a familiar word in the hoardings
Walk on keep your strangeness unsensed
You residence papers will do you no good
You're in the city of your birth

Song Of The Wearers Of Second-Hand Clothes

Once you grow tired and throw off bought dreams
Don't look back
Because I'm there.
A dream of kissing in moonlight
A worn velvet blouse embroidered with silver thread
A honeymoon renewed with lacey suspenders
It's no use now... I'm getting cold.
My dreams
Need something warm.

A half-finished soup
A steak returned and "betrayal" is foreign to me
Not the slender heels of your summer clogs
I need something thick and washable
I need something as known to me as my family
And colour, it must have colour for sure
To cover my wear and tear.

In your markets there is no cloth for sale
Which when I touch brings back to mind my childhood
But won't disclose the secrets of my youth.
Your clothes were not tailored to my pain.
But you know that dread.
To grow old and be deserted.
I have many kinds
But they do not fit with yours
Most of mine are born of love.

All my money can afford at this stall
Are the second-hand clothes you sell
And when my hand touches them they breathe new life
But are you the one worn out?

War Doesn't Separate Lovers

A mere step from blind bullets
At my cigarette's trembling tip
I taste your kiss like a knife

Pebbles shied away
From our feverish loving madness
Dawn was a vast roar
Almost setting the sea aflame

A blade whetted to its limit
Now we recall the day of loving
Our kisses are cold and sharp
The wedding like a subtle ache

To your hands a mere step
A mere step from blind bullets
I taste your kiss like a knife

Dreams

I

With joy
The telephone rang
The house's loneliness
Rang paused
The telephone
Curious
Anxious
Shouted

Shouted
Stopped

The bed stays folded to one side
The coverless quilt
The pillow slipped to the floor
A curtain stained with hand prints
Become threadbare causes night to trickle out
A single slipper facing the wrong way
At the foot of the wall

In the half-dark
The telephone rings
As if it wants to wake us
Hurriedly
Once again
Calling out
Sobbing
Sobbing

II

Why does rain
Bring desert to mind
And what separates
Beach from desert

Visions
Search for a remedy
With drying tears
Of nights

On the shore
Perhaps

It's the footprint
That didn't reach the sea
That now is wetted

Far away
In the desert
The dead child's eyelashes
Are scattered

Rain
Brings desert to mind
Its worry

III

The seagull's cry glided around
"Ruined.. The City ruined.. ruined.."
On the tip of the last opening branch
The quince blossom felt ashamed
"The weight…"
Asphalt bubbled underfoot
Undulated
Settled

"Ruined… ruined…"
The seagull
Wheeling around
On the horizon

Dreams and Wings

Mouth of a volcano maybe
Or maybe hell
Resembling the mouths of baby sparrows
A cloud of a thousand birds
Born at the same moment
From a flaming egg
Fluttering their wings together
Choking in the vapour

Their feathers like tears
Damp
Is this why they can't raise them
Their wings
Or don't
Don't they have any wings

Birds
That crack-open the volcano's mouth
And the flaming egg

Leave them
Let them fly.

Sennur Sezer

from Sullied Papers

I

Do you know those waiting rooms in small stations?
In evening hours, to distant Istanbul, Ankara, the World,
Darkness suddenly descends. And now you're always late,
The smell of smoke pervading you.

The body weary for sleep, the smell of bitter oil and something
Unknown all around. It's clear the mail has long since gone.
And the fast well-lit train won't stop here. You came too late.

A rumour animated everyone: "The Winter solstice
Will return before the fires of the Summer solstice are out.
The crocus and the early fruits will disperse in the blizzard…
Plumb blossoms will retreat…" The wild ungrowing pear
Says again: "Winter solstice will return…" And beneath
Its thick outer skin it hides its pleasurable taste…

Women, whose absence is only sensed. Women,
A simple veil, a colour, a movement… As common
As ants… Their lot in life, no greater than ants. Migrants,
Who don't know trains. In a loneliness without cypress
Or willow, syllable stones all in a row.

Waiting rooms. Cheap tobacco, a mail sack,
And a story: in faint light. The door of dry, lightless villages.
To those who see this world as a brief stop, who say: "This
Is where your lot falls. Wait…" And in the sky
There's a flock of migrant cranes, already late.

I say, do you know those waiting rooms?

Gülseli İnal

Gülseli İnal was born in Istanbul in 1947. She started writing at an early age and read Philosophy at Istanbul University. A tireless innovator, her *Collected Poems*, published by Yasakmeyve in 2009, runs to more than four volumes. Her poems have been translated into every major European language.

An Astral Moment

Stormy springs touched
As small
Mistakes begin
Lilies
Rising
From the sand's body
As if
Like this, a ruler of sand
Hidden
With astral awakening
And an asteroid sea

Sigma

I

Wine coloured sea
Trees
Completely orange
The eagle sweeps down
          and changes the course of rivers
It binds both banks
Its feathers become a bridge
Its long beak a passage
Just then
A flock of birds
From a magical land
Fills the earth and sky
Sending out
An endless
Warning
All sparkling things
Meet in air

II

A sigma parallel to ground
Between green branches
Is putting on the wind
Smitten
With spring roses
Swimming in Rahia,
The circle's sole centre

Defying the word of God
Stems
stoop
Colour bends its head

Your face is in roses
Fog veils your body
Thin body
Roots fed from the voice
Gush
From the ground
Marble is split
From pure white
The Judas Tree descends

Yeast

I

The farthest star is my friend
Light
The most talkative from afar
When light dies
In my body's theory
Night murmurs
A woman appears
Her eyes pulled towards seas
The full moon
Or else
Pearls
As big as the full moon
Or teardrops
Break into life

In their nest
A girl arrives
With blonde curls,
Strokes linen-white hair,
Dances,
And from now on no yeast will form

II

Because I love
God's colours
The uterus is blue
The blood flowing in green
The red words
And
The secret death
In purple
Poured away
Transmutable
Collected
In the wells of the world

Elliptical Bird

I

After a storm my hands
Feel the tower
With the shadow of a huge beast
The shadow retreats
I touch the elliptical fruit
Suddenly ripening on the branch
Crimson anger

With the pure colour of coral
Suddenly given
And taken
Back
With the seed growing inside

II

I listened to its breath
With that saddening contrary tongue
At the point where we met
Pirate grasses used to grow
And then
The black grape's dirge
Became your song
You were noted there
Among those illicit grasses
The moment
You undressed
And night burned
With a white wish
How come
This
Wet clay
Gave us
Back
Faces reshaped again
Our voices mixed with black
White blended in
Some dream travelers
Appeared at the mountain peak
The gypsy season
Left its unreturned dead on the patio

Zerrin Taşpınar

Zerrin Taşpınar was born in Ankara in 1947. Although she began writing at an early age, it was only in the 1980's that her poems, stories and essays began to appear with regularity. She was one of only thirty-five people to survive the infamous *Madımak Incident* on 2 July, 1993, in which a hotel in Sivas, hosting a conference of left-wing writers and intellectuals, was deliberately set alight.

September in Demetevler Park I

It's around noon
the empty hours of those waking late
those on leave, or jobless ,
those with clothes once fashionable
which now look old and cheap
—showing all the signs of a consumer society—
we pass over the asphalt.

Behind me
a girl carrying sorrow in her heartbeat
the smile of a bud smashing the ice
as if left here for today by a deer.

September in Demetevler Park II

The last swallows will leave this city
Boredom will stream out, old age
Tired from the weight of summer on its back
Demetevler Park
with its colored poles and benches will fade.

My shaky, incompetent steps
As if shamed by their womanhood
—really why when we walk alone
do we frown
and stare at the floor.

September in Demetevler Park III

It's around noon
now there are kitchen sounds in houses.
Turning my back to 16-floor shanties
I want to sate my gaze
in the blue pool of the park.

Three men on a bench
twist their thick black whiskers
and suddenly the urge is gone…

What didn't the water take…

What a clumsy love it was that spoilt Marmara
How did I diminish
Still the fish with silver scales
beneath my skin lived on.

Zerrin Taşpınar

September in Demetevler Park IV

It's around noon
in a thousand years of human history
what does one life matter?
A drop of water
maybe a red flower in a park.

Every season ends
every September… just as it began…

İnci Asena

İnci Asena was born in Istanbul in 1948. For many years she was the director of Adam Publishing, one of Turkey's most prominent poetry publishing houses.

You Didn't Understand

There's something you didn't understand

I left understanding to my child
For he will come naked into this world

It was the twentieth of all the centuries that confused you
A segment of time bound by faith
And it was here that you didn't understand
It was a day determined by the sun
On our blue planet

I left understanding to my child
That he might know his time
***

This is a poem of hope, you didn't understand,
One I have sown into wombs.

Quantum Theory

Quantum theory tum tum tum tum
In a dinner jacket allah lah lah
Do re mi fa sol
La ilahi dolce vita
Crows are laughing
Thinking of the one doing evil
"Porchu polunu selinka (what do they want to do)?"

Alone in a separate dimension
Taking potassium, lithium, calcium from the earth
Making love with sun and air
Far from humankind
Far from humankind
Very unlike humans

***

On the first day.
A beautiful sunny day
An apple in my hand beneath the tree
I lounged about all day
After strolling around with my island
River mountain plane
Every climate, each single one

Each plant
Each animal, except for monkeys.

The second day. Morning.
Yesterday I experienced the Neolithic age
I'll taste the Paleolithic too
Crusoe built a house I'll build one too
I'll take fire from Prometheus, easy
I should fish today too.

The second day. Evening.
I was thoroughly exhausted
Happy as a child I caught fish.
A stool, a table, and a leather sandal
I came upon evening.

The third day.
I went to my island's pole to cool down
I ought to pass quickly to the Bullet Age
And find myself a pelt.
Leopard.
The Leopard was a handful but the lamb

Was worth all the trouble,
If only there was wine
Tomorrow I must make wine.

The fourth day.
I listen to the music of nature – my head a little foggy
Knowing each particular sound – my head befuddled
"The smoke-wrapped mountain stones"
My black-eyed, green-eyed, hazel-eyed, purple-eyed lovers
For each I'll give a separate place in my dreams.

The fifth day.
I assign the plane-tree as your slave Beethoven
The cherry to you, Chopin
And the whole weight of the rainforest to Mozart
And one by one I hand them out.

The sixth day.
There are no monkeys.
If only there were monkeys.

The seventh day.
Hitler, I will admit even you
You commit evil
And I adjudicate.
They put a hole in the ozone
And we stitch it up.
As they push people apart
We proliferate love.

***

Quantum theory tum tum tum tum
With this rough faith I'm becoming human.

Ayten Mutlu

Ayten Mutlu was born in Balıkesir in 1952. She graduated from Istanbul University's School of Business Administration and later studied in the Civil Engineering Faculty at Yıldız Technical University. Her essays, short stories and poems have been widely published. She won the İbrahim Yıldızoğlu Poetry Prize in 1997 and the Yalova International Poetry Prize in 2001.

Wind

woman smaller than a grain of sand
the sea smaller still than a woman's pain

it came and went that ancient wind
ignoring the sea and the Milky Way

and the woman walked with her naked memories
never stepping on the sand or the stars

People

Small homes between earth and sky
rooms murmuring, windows ajar
pots and pans, chairs, a worn out table
tiny habits, and stale tastes
a handful of dust, an afternoon shadow
and time sitting back on its corner seat

between walls known to each other
what possessions, what anguish, what little love
a fragment of salt picked from the sea, from the sun
a carefree feeling, a kiss, a laugh
whispers, vapour of flowers in the vase
and in the moments' haste
the pervasive smell of death

a mass of souls between earth and sky
a goblet of rage, an ocean of grief
screams, pleas, profound silence
and through the veins of these small houses
pulsing and flowing
and flowing on
this longing for life

Your Face and the Tolling of Bells

to laugh with you was like spring
to touch the tolling bells of your face
sensual and calm like a naked pomegranate

your face was the sign of late morning

in autumn's usual haunt
in your face's closed seas
birds flew like poisoned arrows
summer was blindfolded at the foot of a wall

what remained of your face, a rusted shadow
a receding forest, a flower in mourning
fragments of glass in the colours of spring

how do birds get used to losing a sky?

oh, how late I was to learn of rain
like a naked pomegranate, broken and torn
in the place where your old face, like decaying autumn,
wasted away with the tolling of bells

Oya Uysal

Oya Uysal was born in 1952 in Istanbul. She is the author of four collections of poetry and a recipient of the Cemal Süreya Poetry Prize.

The Shoreless River

Everyone turns again to themselves with their own sorrow.
Evening, disappearing in night's shadows.

I too looked into the mirror of your heart, your face
                                        growing pale,
a picture that doesn't seek its source.

                    Oh! The changing season of your soul.
Even when your disdainful smile makes you unreachable,
Self-sufficiency now is a desire for shelter.

You're the child skimming letter on water. A deep and
                                        bygone language,
a river without a shore…

Everyone turns again to themselves with their own sorrow.
Evening, disappearing in night's shadows.

The Smell of Faded Things

A life scattered in its own wind, this life of mine,
mundane, quiet, barely visible.

As days multiply by days my city is now an empty house,
and the street is rain
                              in the eyes
of an orphan.

                  So it changed its place with grief,
sorrow making a place in my destitute soul.
The cat brushing against my shirt went home,
the smell of faded things, goose bumps,
                                        evening!
if I could lie down and sleep and someone cover me.

A life scattered in its own wind, this life of mine,
mundane, quiet, barely visible.

Room with the Curtain Drawn

Night woke to the sound of a dream sobbing, a delicate sound,
night descending into sleep about me.

I observed life and myself as if I were someone else
from the outside
the pale yellow lights of my room from afar
my vision of my brow pressed to the cold glass

the lover I watch in my mind's eye.

You, who are my nothing and my everything
                the one tormenting me
in this love I fear to lose
                with my disappearing body
Now I'm a room with the curtains drawn.

Night woke to the sound of a dream sobbing, a delicate sound,
night descending into sleep about me.

Leyla Şahin

Leyla Şahin was born in Şavşat, near Artvin, in 1954. She was educated in Istanbul at the Üsküdar College for Girls. She has worked for many years as a journalist, writing for such papers as *Cumhuriyet* and *Millet*. She won the Enver Gökçe Poetry Prize in 1988.

Broken Windows

we're hopeful migrants
we pitch our tents in the open
now open your arms
a bird multiplies in air

we're a raised voice
we rise with our eyelashes wet
put your arms around me
it's love that rears the day

our eyes and brows cast down
walk now through roses, sweat
(windows broken
you can't take me away from sorrow
it's only for you that I cry)

a bird multiplies in air
my eyes overrun my eyes
I'd have been as mute as stone, but for you.

In Love with the Wind

alone, and alone before too
from his eyes a carnation clings on to the world
in the middle of that world he was alone.

his kite never once reached the clouds
in the middle of that world he was alone.

the sun never once warmed his heart
in all the winters there were he was alone.

he lived a timid, fearful life
alone, alone among voices.

in his vision and his pose he was alone
in his memories alone, he had no songs:
in the evening he was most alone…

The Smile of Love

so here I am, coming to you
find for me a place on wings of soft winds
let water's sparkling sounds flow beside us,
let laurels entwine our flanks...
let me wake on mornings in the softness of your iron arms
as a seed grows in the eyes of an olive tree
let me be yours

let the scent of the gum tree infuse our hair
let our living body walk towards birds
and find forgotten songs...
your smile is the branches of a flowering almond tree
let it snatch death from our hands.

I brought a ship to your door: let's go together.
you were made for women of sensitive, long nights,
for long mornings
for fields of wheat, placid deer, for open roads...
drop me on your chest: let me listen to songs of the world
if we're late, the quiet river of love will leave us —sulking—
and never come back again.

Aslı Durak was born in Istanbul in 1955. She was educated at the Kadıköy College for Girls and later graduated from the Faculty of Architecture, Mimar Sinan University, Istanbul. She is a member of the Turkish Writers Association.

A Windless Poppy

Touched-leaves still on the floor
It danced with wind
Swayed in her bloody shawl
Wind cut dead
And the dance half-done
In coarse, dark rasping pain
The poppy sheds its leaves

Pale Blue

Hold my hand
Not to carry me far away... no.
My roots and branches
Will strain for distant clouds

Maybe my eyes
Are in that same pavilion of loneliness now
Let my face again be the statue of sadness

When you beautify me
Maybe
I'm a pale blue woman now

Lâle Müldür

Lâle Müldür was born in 1956 in Aydın, and is one of Turkish poetry's most eccentric stylists. She holds degrees from the University of Manchester and Essex University, in England, and spent several years living in Belgium. A collection of her poems was translated at the Tyrone Guthrie Centre, Ireland, and published in 1998 as *Water Music* by Poetry Ireland.

Mary Incense

I

Every angel is cruel. Those 13 months
Bound by Mary's cord. I don't know why
Those terrible angels kept us apart
That 'year of 13 moons.' I met you
In my melancholy's 19th week. It was as if some things
Suddenly changed.
As if for now I no longer drag

This thing called fate before that rabid horse.
Then a terrible sleet poured down.
Frightening winds blew. The star of the Southern Cross
Stirred in its place. It was the 19th week of my melancholy.
Every angel sees what comes before us and
After us. It was out of our hands.
That year of 13 moons kept us apart.
Why does my love start things that will come to an end,
Why does a Mohammedi rose grow all of a sudden
Why does hail fall the size of tears?
On a black satin abaya
I'm drawing a golden cross for you.
In this way I can explain your absence now.
I'm opening my eyes wide apart
To the wind of angel-blown splinters
Of glass. You're not coming. Jet black horses
Come to my cold room. Descending meteors
Come. Angels come with eyes bound
In darkness. You're not coming.
There's no reason. No reason at all.
In churches girls pray to icons
For us. Outside a terrible sleet
That pulls at our rope, more terrible
Than all the angels. I just don't know
Maybe we committed some awful sin.
I wrap myself in my monastic cloak.
13 months will pass in this way. The Star
of the Southern Cross will grin at us darkly.
I'll sing songs my tongue can't turn.
A spell begun I've no idea by who
Or why will flow from my zenith
The year of 13 moons.
I'll want to wash my hands,
Perhaps turn back.
But I won't be able to return.
The year of 13 moons will flow

Over that dark sheet with its golden cross.

O sole mio! O Sole Negre!

II

Not even St. George could kill
The insoluble love in me.
Famous glum-faced Michael
With his angels
Pointlessly coming to my aid.
Silence! Soul-life!
I pass my days in silence
As if cleansed in the waters of Ayazma
I know in April the jug will crack
Did you ever think what else might happen?
The Angel and the Devil press into
The hearts of men and leave something…
Silence! Soul-life!
Everything should be kept as a vast religious secret
Yes, nothing on lips
No frozen smile nor
Even Ameshas Spentas' angels
Should reveal what's hidden
There's no need for me to sob before the rabbi
Only pray, I'm praying.
Yes, maybe tomorrow, tomorrow
Everything might change
Pearls of Mourning and those bound to the Angel of Rome
Will withdraw
Shhhh, yes, even this is too much!
Silence! Soul-life! Didn't you ever think?

"And Adam loved God
And woman loved Adam loving God."

III

It's obvious, they will try to destroy us
With this clear dark conspiracy
Casting ill omen'd glances before my house
As if they don't know what's going on
Narrowing their eyes like owls
Shhh! Silence! Soul-life!

'O my people, what have I done unto thee.'

'Great star of the Sisters of Love' Mary,
Expecting no visitor
Was caught in her damp towel by Gabriel
They too are amongst us
Caught in our warm glances
Like a wet towel or a negligee

It's her, but remember me, remember me
I washed your feet
Your muddy, sinful feet
'Ricorditi di me, che son la pia;
Ricorditi di me.'

O my people.

Lâle Müldür

IV

"Apricot blossom
blowing from East to West,
I tried to stop the falling."

Summer passed quickly with long-necked lutes
A raspberry rain is coming down now
Grandfather sleeping inside
In that wet raspberry country
      the Jerusalem Virgins' elegy begins.

Summer passed quickly with sudden downpours
The woman dozing off on her prayer rug
She is a raspberry country now
In her heart an angry and terrifying
song begins.

Did I want to go back
Did I want to go back
To being without you,
      to that pagan country

To return with rock and roll songs behind me
To return dressed in decadent and coquettish
                           Venetian clothes
To return to a heap of my waiting flirts
CONTRA NATURA

And to say   'I am Lazarus
                Back from the land of the dead
                Forgive me'

Forgive me among you
                For the terrible things I've seen
For distancing myself from you
With violets in my hand
                Forgive me

I want to mix with Jerusalem Virgins
In that wet raspberry land
I want to give birth to a boy
                And forget you.

V

Recall too Mary's episode from The Book.
On that day the angels spoke thus:
"O Mary, truly Allah chose you,
Purified you and raised you above
All the nations' women of your age."
Or else you were not beside them
When they cast their fates
To see who'd be Mary's protector.
Dark conspirators alone with their glasshouse dreams
Said: "O Mary, who are you

What an extraordinary thing you've done,
O sister of Hârun,
Your father wasn't a bad man,
Your mother wasn't a whore."
On this Mary winked at Jesus.
On this Mary winked at Jesus.

Imran's daughter, Mary, her mother Hannah!
First among the women of Heaven!
Poor Mary! Always thinking!
When her hair wavers in the wind, poor young Mary!
"What would it matter
If I'd died long before I'd seen these days…"
She was never this lonely before.
"So who are you, Mary?
Queen! Queen!"

This is the Mary episode we discussed.
They should know the day they'll see angels
There will be no good news
On that day for sinners

Except for Mary and her son,
To all newborn infants
Satan extends a hand
And that's why they cry
As soon as they're born

VI

Melancholy love!
Memorabilia!

"…the Angel wanted to stay on…
But the storm blasting from Heaven
Took hold of its wings with such force
It could not fold them again."

Angel of history
Face turned to the past,
Helpless in the storm,
Dragged forward into the future…

Attaining a girlhood as good as new
Untouchable like Eurydice.

And suddenly,
God, holding her hand, with a painful
Scream, spoke these words: "He looked back!" —
She understood nothing, and asked quietly: "Who?"

VII

Irhâç: light of her forefathers' brow

On the brow of Mary's forefathers
A word was written in code: MHMD

They are an inbred race!

Mary's pearl birth
It's said the oyster sometimes rises to the surface
Draws rain into itself like a heavenly seed
It's said pearl is good for melancholy
Unpierced, virgin pearls…

VIII

Maryan Al Basriya
Was in the service of Rabia Al Adawiya:
She fainted when she heard
God's science of love.

In a dervish trance
She died of love…

God has servants who resemble rain.
They fall on soil becoming corn, they fall in sea becoming pearl.

IX

The universe is a compound of four elements
Whichever you choose, you start to blossom

Rose: burns in fire
        dries without water
        chokes without air
        freezes in marble

X

In my dream at night on a train I boarded as a runaway
I was searching for sea salt. Salt and a white horse!
The image of Jesus! For salt, which lends taste to everything,
To create itself is impossible. At last I understand
The dark conspiracy. Just like Nerval
I too preferred the created to the Creator.
To forget my terrible regrets, with visions of love and death,
I took to walking in wide open meadowlands.
As Nerval is in church asking forgiveness before the image
Of Poor Dead Mary, and as his ring
Inscribed with the name of Allah, Mohammed and Ali
Falls to the floor, suddenly all the candles light up
And the Ave Maria begins.
On the mountains of the Himalayas a tiny flower
Blooms. Don't forget me!

XI

A mystic strange thing
Meeting like this
Maybe because we've met before

I stretch out wrapped in an old fur
In the room now / thinking of you
Doors windows forms
Softening disappearing
White clouds crowding the room
Above the clouds a moment
I seem to fly
I'm touching something light scary

A thigh perhaps
        A white horse stirring into life
        An incomplete piece
A dust cloud
In its original state
A horse on the brink of creation!

Or maybe I was passing through an angel…

XII

Wherever I look I encounter the red mark of sin.
Easterners westerners northerners southerners feudalists
Aristocrats bourgeois businessmen artists toasters
Jews Christians Muslims. The pearl is the genius
Thinking at night inside the oyster, my last utopia
Like a community of Muslims. And yet they also break apart
Like a broken pearl necklace.
Wherever I look I encounter the red mark of cruelty.
I declared the end of the world had come and became
A cold, cold woman, a Lady d'Arbanville.
                A FLOWER THAT SUDDENLY CLOSES
                JUST AS IT'S ABOUT TO BLOOM
                I BECAME AN APACHE AT THE START OF
LOVE
AND A MEDIEVAL LADY
                WITH A CHASTITY BELT AT THE END
YES BUT WHAT A SHAME WHAT A SHAME BUT
FROM A WARM-BLOODED GIRL LIKE ME THE WORLD
CREATED A LADY D'ARBANVILLE
YES BUT WHAT A SHAME WHAT A SHAME FOR ME

STILL I'M JUSTLY PROUD
SLEEPING IN MY COLD BED WITH THE QUARTZ SIGN
        OF MY CHASTITY UPON MY HEAD

O LADY MARY, LADY OF THE LILLIES
ON SNOWY MEDIEVAL NIGHTS GATHER ME TO YOUR
SIDE…

Nilgün Marmara

Nilgün Marmara was born in Istanbul on 12 February, 1958. She graduated from Boğaziçi University with a thesis on Sylvia Plath. She committed suicide on 13 October 1987. Her poems were published posthumously.

Pink Lover

O, that's how it was!
He lived in a cat cage,
As real as evil,
He would laugh at the world,
Again and again.

Pink lover
In the nursery of insanity.
With tears as false as art
He would cry at the world,
Again and again—

November, 84

Family

Death turned home
From poisoned roses
With its two breasts.
Blood dripping
         blood
         from the tips

—A calm sleep's
         first stirrings—

My lonely gaze
         is given up
         to any old rainbow's fall,
Gazing at the innocent will
         of a violent cyclone:

Let there not be mourning!

Let there be no mourning!

August, 82

Body

His body is a lunatic asylum
Busy hands inside, crazy and diligent!

His body is a tower.
So many steps inside, dark and damp.
He takes you up laughing,
He brings you down in tears!

His body is a globe.
Its surface all mystery, bright and fluid.
Shows, revealing as he turns
Respectful of time, and pitying…

May, 86

My Bird and I…

My bird and I are asleep
In a mirror, our cage is our bed
our faces seen in each other
we sleep beneath endless snow
my bird and I
my spouse and I are bound
by a crimson thread
its undoing, destitutions delight.

In our mirror, this single bond...
This crimson link my equal my bird and I...

Child

Compliant hand
        —being held—
of a child.
No image in the two-way mirror
        —if you should look—

Rough sea draws breath
        like a human
            —dispensing—
to the child's pale skin
        its bitter blue.

The timid child
Forsakes his two shoes
For a very singular death.

April, 82

Crimson Lake

Blood Mirror,
Post-tristesse buried in its treasure chest

its secret,

Red oval, plunges into the eye of those that ignore it.

You, Him, me,
One day we were part of the lake's wide-reaching
net,
When suddenly the weed grew hideously
Encircling and entwining us.

It is dark, and the power is there,
To strip us naked once more,
To bath us in that crimson lake.

March, 81

Neşe Yaşın

Neşe Yaşın was born in 1959 to Turkish Cypriot parents. She graduated from Middle East Technical University, in Ankara, and currently works at the University of Cyprus, in Nicosia. She plays an active role in Cypriot politics.

On A Rope

I

My wounded bird
my phoenix risen from its ash
would see only a dark abyss
when it gazed upon the world
uncles made crazy by war
walking towards suicide
with regular steps

my phoenix
would die and be born again
when eclipsed by a new woman

Neşe Yaşın

II

Poetry became the village idiot
banging a tin can
to your old lines
dancing and turning naked
in your sacred shrines
(martyrs were returning to life
and weeping
over their youthful portraits)
everyone taken up with their own dream

III

When I tripped and scuffed
my knees in this game of love
he would kiss them

I loved it but
it was something I couldn't bare
in this form of a women

IV

Its voice
as it weeps like a damaged flute
in that crazy dance with death
love was a lorry we got into hitchhiking
as the old driver told his moving tales
we were racing hell for leather into darkness
everybody taken up with their own dream

V

I'm afraid to admit it but
in an earthquake's fury I fell in love
by crippling myself forever

Just watching him would be enough
but he opens his mouth and a poem opens
a fire is made when he touches

VI

His eyes full of verses
are whispering forests of wind
shiftless waves of hair

He was an acrobat of love
undaunted by the rope

VII

Where he'd pass
the naked bodies of women
everyone made him infamous
only poetry and I knew
the mystery of goodness he had.

Dream

A chilled soul
seeking warmth
a women imprisoned
in her own tower
in questions and riddles
looks to each face of the passengers

You are the only place where you cannot be seen
in the error of lying mirrors

Not to another city
to go to another person
maybe this is how the dream
will live, or die like this

Perihan Mağden

Perihan Mağden was born in Istanbul in 1960. Better known as a novelist and newspaper columnist, she was described by Orhan Pamuk as "one of the most inventive and outspoken writers of our time". Her only book of poems, *Mutfak Kazaları*, was published in 1995. A translation of her celebrated novel, *İki Genç Kızın Romanı*, was published as *Two Girls* by Serpent's Tail in 2005.

Worldly Affairs

I've taken the dust off the dust
That beast of a vacuum in the corner:
"Come here and I'll throttle you."
I bend my neck and from my mouth
Spew pieces of sponge on the floor

One side of the fridge is thick dust

There's always someone asleep inside
There's always someone waking inside
The mound of dry laundry is like an insolent gut:

"Fold us, tuck us, put us neatly away,"
It says, baring its teeth at me

One side of the fridge is thick dust

The set of knives, sure of its treachery:
"Soon your blood will grace our bodies,
you idiot, you always cut your hands"
Don't let the past boil over
I won't clean the cooker again.

One side of the fridge is thick dust

Dust and particles in plastic bottles
Ready to make their best of me:
"Pour out, scratch off, end it; bring a new one!"
Fragments on the floor, coquettish, flirtatious
"Come on, then, catch me if you can."

Onions, carrots, potatoes, celery, parsley
And squash should be nicely chopped up;
A spoonful of semolina, one of rice, a little
Oil; lightly stir over a low heat
There is a beautiful purple vein on my wrist.

Clean panties and bra under
My tight jeans and jumper
How far might I fall from the balcony
Were I to gather my hair into a ball
I hope my clothes stay put when they take me away

The terrace still needs a clean,
Pillows fluffing, towels hanging,
The bin needs a wash
And mind the branches when you jump
When wiping down the window.

One side of the fridge

Morning in Maduray

Didn't I tell you
Not to open your mouth
Not to swallow birds
Their wings flap inside
And tire you.

They're woken before dawn
On trains
The bags under your eyes grow bigger
Listening to songs in temples
You unwind.

The Seventh Step

I'm a black forgotten bag at the station
I'm in tears but no one sees
I spit daylight into night
Istanbul nights stink of men

In the sky, blue mounts its greatest fight
Night presses against the sea, raping it
How your hands twist my heart
I close my windows but it's useless

I'm the ten thousand children sworn to night
I'm the wild apricot twig robbed of hope
On the sixth step I hold you tight
On the seventh, we part…

Perihan Mağden

Kitchen Catastrophes

Turn the knobs. Turn them all.
But that towel is clean. Fine.
An unlucky princess printed on it.
Wet it. The unlucky princess is sobbing.
Plug it under the door
What a small kitchen
How did we ever fit in. I and they, side by side.
I'm stuffed. And bored stiff.
Yesterday too. And that day on holiday.
Season of Fry-ups. Pickles. Rain.
Dust. Dust. Ever-moving-duster.
On the shopping list. No, it wasn't.
Hey princess! I bought you
In a sale. But god, I loved you.
Not a single day did you go unironed.
Cold fish swim in your eyes.
"We made your throne but not your fortune"
Those were words well said mother.
I've never like that saying. And a
Whole heap of others.
The wound on my left index finger
Keeps on swelling. Hot water
Makes it worse. I know.
The stairs go up. And so do I, on the stairs.
My stairship. String the ocean
And hang it around my neck. I'm getting cold
Climbing step by step
My arms darkening
My eyes sinking within me
My stairs of gas. My gas stairs.
Leak. Leaks. Leaking. Run. Run. Runnn.
Away from here. Hey away

Flower Question

I know, you have jobs to do,
It's your job to get holiday mornings underway
To push kids back and forth on swings of love,
To wave them off to gardens of the heart

I know, you have jobs to do
You're knitting frousty warmths in your hands
Your hands burn, you feel sick
I know, you have jobs to do

You have wood of the forest weathercock to find
You have the balloon from beyond the hill to inflate
You have the world to teach these songs of grace
Kids should be at ease to laugh out loud

I know, you have jobs to do
If I poured out a pan of scalding water
If the clouds suddenly were to draw over my eyes
If I could ask again and want even more
Would you come to the corner with me?

Birds

Deceitful stones these birds
Recalling spring, they sing of it
Morning I opened the window
Winter streets, spring birds

Perihan Mağden

Nebahat, Where Are You Coming From

Osman you'll never know how bad I am
I kiss the lips of wineglasses
                              and of men
Like a painted bird slipping into the night
I'm treacherous for you

High heeled shoes,
                    you know I'm short
And I put on my purple skirt
I keep on smiling and singing
Osman you've no idea the woman I am

Men always hungry, open, ready for me
Shame I've never got rid of these habits
I can't say no to anyone
Wherever they drag me, I go

Osman I swear I've a heart of gold
I don't know, suddenly I miss you
And when your dark eyes fall down
Into my heart, I feel ashamed

Osman forgive me. Or else don't.
Look I'm an honest woman, really
Take my hand. I won't go again
I love you for all the world.

Çiğdem Sezer

Çiğdem Sezer was born in the Black Sea city of Trabzon in 1960.
She studied in Ankara and later worked for many years as a college
teacher in Sakarya. She has won several major awards for her poetry,
including the Arıburnu Poetry Prize in 1998 and the Ceyhun Atuf
Kansu Poetry Prize in 2006.

Closed City

Intermissions stations platforms
Doors; bang!
Windows curtains
And sometimes words to be quiet

Bedsteads closets drawers; bang!
Tea cracks open in the glass, a book on the table
The stove's tiny flame heats up the darkness
Spoon and soup
Frowning brows affronted table
No one can grasp the soup's steam

Hanging shadow of grape and wine in the vineyard
Turning pot in the kiln kneading mud
It wasn't a dream so why is the world sleepy-eyed?

Is there still a song that starts
Oh my darling dear, oh my two eyes
If so, may god make me blind
I didn't hear, whoever said it it's a lie
Remembering is enough, forget about singing it

The woman picks grapes her hands purple trouble
Which now and then she wears in her gaze
As if the vines might fall between her brows
She isn't crushing the grapes but herself
Then sits and drinks it deep

No one opens their heart or home to the city
Walls; bang!

And then… explosion!...

My Ring Finger

A void left by birds
Call it life, let the hurt linger

We're like this, two of a kind

You were a mountaineer as distant as you go
I too was a snow encrusted peak
And you're a hole as big as forgetfulness

Autumn hurts the skin most
A mark like Autumn on our bodies
I was naked for you, you were mountain-gazing
I fell into myself like a clot

In my garden the camphor tree grows
So that no one may enter
The muezzin calls out to death in his black voice
Above us the sky grows older

Be quiet, for the sake of the fatherless
And for the poor and the deprived
All those savages dance on top of us

This Autumn I was cold and the birds left
Silence became my language
I raised a dark-skinned boy, thinking he was yours

It was Autumn, leaves gathered
My ring finger sank into my heart
For you my garden
Abstraction and snow,
An opened wine bottle
And a cruel dream between us

Zeynep Uzunbay was born in the village of Karaözü, in the province of Kayseri in 1961. She trained first as a nurse in Kayseri and then studied Literature at Gazi University, Ankara. She now lives in Izmir.

The Sleepless

—They made us in the dark

—Obviously
I see you better
When I close my eyes

—Our house is all tiny paper

—Are we memory, Snotty?

—Didn't you like it Snotless?

—Memory won't stay homeless
It finds itself a scab
Whispering wind, dancing fire

—Between two volcanoes
Black rainbows
In those children's skies

—Where are the sons
Testing their fresh beards
In their mothers' palms,
Who part their hair
And smile? Why?

—You are my sweet quiet seed in misty soil,
Let sleep be your house now

—Where's my beauty?
Did it fall off
When I was slapped?

—Whiter than a dove, greener than a parrot
You're pinker than a flamingo
Perch on my black chest
My loved one, my bat

Zeynep Uzunbay

Black Moon

We rubbed our eyes
Looked around, rubbed again
There was no horizon

Sun scraped off its last light
There's a black moon tonight
The sky's voice was silenced

Bored with distant mouths
We'll shape our long words
To our own tongues
Secret as soil's black blood
As a mountain, belly-filled
With silver

Poison water poison sky
Uprooted trees
Without a dying wish
Abandoned wheat
If the child grows at all
He'll be a young corpse

Let's catch a chill
And rub two stones together
Even if we can't recall our first promise
Let the dwarf star split on
That shameless place, on our face

Our Word

Everything resembles us
We're two pine-nuts
Sharing our water, listen
Whatever wind says is true

> *I'm a little paranoid peanut,*
> *Groans hollow my curves without cause*

Word, our cherished one:
Opens its beak to the sky
A cloud? Moon? Come evening
We plop a lilac sea into its mouth

> *A dead-calm, pale longing*
> *A mast, a prow...*

He knows what it is to love:
The weight of my soul, the clever
Cock who reads our every thought
Everything! Everything!

> *Slipping stubbornly into silence*
> *Stay nameless, stay alone!*

Saying, let it go
Fall, linger on, find
Let it know we have our word

> *Word, don't forget us!*

Betül Tarıman

Betül Tarıman was born in Keşan, Edirne, in 1962. She graduated from Hacettepe University, Ankara, with a degree in History. A widely published poet, she won the prestigious Necatigil Prize in 2004. She lives in Antalya.

Moon Hunter

(Actor)

I'm worried
My neck sweaty, my loins
Beneath me the sheets' rustle
Inside me the aging girl
Her moth-eaten desires

Sometimes a scent
Of roses opens in me
A light breeze on my shirt
Love is like the place it was born

My skin: clear water, my skin: voracious bird
Its mouth pink, simple, innocent
                              Saying is important

Even if they think of me as a child
In that place I come from
Now I'm diffident
Dilapidated skin
Behind the stage
                              I drowned as I struggled

(Spectator)

A street always smiles
A house seeks a friend
Grieved and remorseful
Someone silent downtrodden
Tells of the place where water bled

Wherever I look is a mirror
Inside my torn insides
How many women, post-natal
A pain deep within me
As I look let my mirror be my joy
I said
Let the mountain hope for me
Let love hope for me

(Mirror)

The one left in the night closed like a box
Time's terrible roar
Chilling the walls
                              As if angrily
                              Throwing a stone in water
                              I knew how to gauge its sorrow

Betül Tarıman

Songs are the Joy of Overflowing Wine

Love might one day come
I was compelled to love's sorrow
Love is a junkman
Songs keep his door ajar
My drunken depths have no end
Throw me a rose
Songs are a pretext
For me to love

Sad farewells are companions to song
And grey and red
Set down sorrow between two seasons
My god I'm cold
If the street should close about me

Love can one day go
Its geography is wooden
It might burst into forgetfulness
It has a house forbidden to itself
The game it plays with death
Is a long one "rosebud"

Rebellion

I was a child
I gathered a lake for the plain
My mother pressed silk into bloom
My father came too, wounded horses in my dream

Mother, bury me in your sleep
In your pearl
Life is cloth rotting
There's a horse galloping inside me
As free of reins
As the children you raised

From the coolness of narrow mountain roads
From the fusty smell of old cities
I'm in love as if I were twenty-four
I became one of time's embers
S m i l i n g
My father came too

My mother who dressed me in her joy

Birhan Keskin was born in Kırklareli in 1963. She is one of the most celebrated poets of the younger generation who has been described as "a major gift to the language." A selection in English, *& Silk & Love & Flame*, is published in the Arc Visible Poets Series.

Leaf

I was tired…
waiting for death with my wuthering roots
summer over
an earth tremour sounding
from roots of the leaf-shedding tree.

I gave birth to you…
from my inner spring, my bitter flow
I gave birth to you, for a dream
from a season on loan.

Glacier

My life passes on water's back
my cities, my palaces, worn out.

Apparently roses are sown in the world
locks are shed on the pillow.
The great depth, eternal, and
low lying, is shifting in me,
turning
a thick fluid: memory.

(A lake touched me in my dream.)

Oh, the wide silence of distance upon me,
a flaking dusk.
Did I live those ages or didn't I
in me, the ashen and endless web of ice.

Who cleaved me, who was my love?
Who shed my blood,
I don't know
I don't recall.
I'd come into the world to ride horses,
was it late March, or February,
roses were being sown in earth,
my blood?

Plain

My two sides, rising mountains, chilled by their grandeur.
One step more to the sun, one step more
one more still… I became broader
now I'm far from myself.

A dried up marsh in my chest
water stands far from my feet.
And I set myself up anew
with silence's echo.

I met with absolute desolation,
I was the absolute detachment from memory.
I'm nothing, me,
pass on.

If the tree will take hold in me, let it trust its roots
if the road will keep on, let it go where it will.
Morning's mist is licking my feet
night too will pass me by.

I shall keep silent.
Let it be how the world will be.

I spread myself, flat on flat, me, I am a plain.
As the wind stirs me, let the grass resound.

Sea

Endlessly I read a rainfall,
carried the wind's long whistle,
posted a letter to a distant shore.
I turned back, beat myself deep inside.
I heard the salt sound broken within me
I cried down to a vast depth.

(A mussel from some sea wavered grief in me,
I saw a stone its weight settled on my tongue)

The boundless sea also pines for distant beyond itself
the horizon says nothing more to me, I saw
love as the texture of a dream
I wanted
the rose's smell, the almond's joy.

Oh nor did I know how vast I was
I wanted to run and to fall into an embrace.

Fig

You made me laugh, Summer, you're my dream
I slept with you, with you I wake.

My insides are soooo big, the world
fits in, next to you.
O my spikeless, cornerless, lingering love
my self as withered as a summer leaf.

Desert

What more is stone than an ember echo?
On earth isn't man just an inclination?

With fires of absence we clung on to being
we cracked and broke
and ached.
Because sand was yellow
the sky, yellow remembrance.

We woke to the earth's harsh knowledge
to bewilderment.
We headed up for the peak from the deep gorge
shedding skin on the road.

The mountain was tongueless, said nothing to us
we looked and pitied our state
- O, our necks weighed us down
we took on loads greater than us.

Desert!
haven't we ached enough
the yellow poison surrounding us
Desert! Lift your sand, feel our plight:

- We're lost in you, where is our way?

Door

Pass through me, I'll remain, I'll wait, pass through me,
but where you pass through me I cannot know.

I was told, there's a ripe fruit behind the curtain of patience,
the world will teach you both patience, and the ripe fruit's taste.

They said, you waited like these trees, a vision like these trees,
sorrowful like these trees.

I was opened, I was closed, opened, closed, I saw
those who went as much as those who came,
where is the end of patience, where the grief stricken ass,
where the audacious fruit,
where is the garden?

If only someone would come… if only someone would see… some-
one had come… opened… stayed
she stays with me still.

For how long this emptiness rings within me, who
slayed the garden's merry widow, the mulberry opposite me?
I glanced with it the most, wanted so much
just once for it to speak.

Were it all up to me I'd have kept quiet longer, yet I creaked wearily,
lest the rusted lock of my tongue be undone,
a stray line somewhere be hummed, the worms inside me crawl.

I saw it all, I saw it all, the end of patience!
if someone would come, would see, would see, now,
the wind is swaying me.

Instrumental

Let it flow, like a black river in me
the entangling grief
whatever I forgot, I try to forget
let it not stay in me
so many inside, the angels
I've gathered from each who left.

If only Time were not so cruel
and I could bring to you that part of me scoured out by sorrow
if the pen would not hold me back, if only I could tell
it's black, Time is a coal black snake
and winter, what won't it do to us.

I declined all sureties, so my heart
might once more trust this dream
black... unchanging
the river within still black
and my heart doesn't understand
why there is no justice?

I am at the fire's burnt out core
that I wrecked and trampled and put out,
inside me, just, as I said
the angels I've gathered from those who left,
a dagger in my heart
once more.

Penguin

Penguin
don't turn your back on me,
I know, I'm like you
and the wind you hold inside.

Penguin
there are things I too hold down inside
glacial shores, screaming memories,
as much as you I'm a fugitive too, and wounded.

Who will forgive me Penguin
I scratched your white and delicate flesh.

One side a blinding brilliant light,
on my other the poisonous night
today I too couldn't climb
on the park swings.
Penguin don't turn your back on me.

I didn't forget the awkward language between us
the world wore us out. I too have things
I couldn't say. And perhaps I'll never say them
you and I, we're coming on a long road,
and along the road I understand, we,
we can't even put a foot on the ground.

Penguin,
who will forgive me?
I scratched your white and delicate flesh
with the thin metal I forgot was in my hand.

Pomegranate Dream

Water for the flower's decreasing water,
we added memory to summer's side,
beneath locust sounds
and the afternoon sun,
we awaited the pomegranate's ripening.

We waited, in different rooms
that the pain we felt might cease,
that it might change into the tiniest ache
like a childhood dream,
we added a pearl-like meaning to summer.

You know,
life goes on like dizziness,
placing one summer next to another,
here time turns into a long heat
into the weight of feeling, into its immovability
and summers into memory…

Will the conversations we shelter in relieve the pain?
Will the sense of the tree's beauty remain,
will love go on in its roots?
My imaginary friend,
this love still owes us:
let the pain we feel in separate rooms cease,
let summer pass and the pomegranate ripen

Bejan Matur

Bejan Matur was born in Maraş in 1968. She was educated in Gaziantep and later studied Law at Ankara University. Two major collections of her verse, *In the Temple of a Patient God* (2004) and *How Abraham Abandoned Me* (2013), appear in Ruth Christie's translations for the Arc Visible Poets Series.

Glacier

In that lake embossed in ice, I was dead a thousand years.
You stirred me.
I awoke and found my sleep in the mist of a burnt forest.
My body fused to night.

A seeping whiteness to the skin from a glacier's deep light
Reminded me;

You walked in that lake.
Leaving skin and a trace.

Libra

I sank in the huge iron boat,
Saw the sea in starlight.
Passing before me a white constellation
Unraveled the language of stars.

And so explained
The why of Polaris hanging there.
And Libra balancing empty space.

For eternity the balance
Weighed with Libra:
If once it tips from its place
The world will be in ruin.

Those Who Seek Out Graves

Those who seek out graves know
Everything made with love is hidden inside
War and skill
Race and grief.

We stopped on an unsealed road.
We were in Antep
In a shadeless field of pistachio trees,
Antep saw everything, grew haggard,
Bare breasted, betrayed.
Like the dream of a shy child
When it rains the earth turns red.

Folk Tale I

I

One snow-filled night
an old storyteller
sat us in a ring
taught us good and bad
by pointing to the fire.
Throughout the dragon's rule
he spun out our childhood,
made it sleep in the garden.

II

What I understood
in that cold,
warm fabled night
was good, the fire I turned my face towards;
bad, the shadow growing on the wall.

Both good
and bad
arose
and died with us.

Folk Tale II

A war goddess
was passing a small wooden bridge,
the snake approaching her sandal
left her untouched.

The soul has no other face
crossing a thin bridge
the bow like a swaying body
lays open entire woods.

Folk Tale III

We know,
the wolf snaps up
a child's opened quilt.
That's what grandmothers are for.
Summer fights on mattresses
who's whose brother
in whose dream does the fairy whisper.

But in those times we were children
whoever had the key was king.

God In The Window

I

Snail that kissed
The neck of my white-eyed god
Sucked his blood.
And my god was then alone.
He knows, my god,
To be kissed like this is to love
And love kills.

II

White eyed
From the window he stares.
Dead white eyes.
He asks "what are you doing"
My shame
Were I to hide my face from him.
My face is his,
His fragile hands.

III

The severed-headed god
Eyes me from my window,
Moulds his face as he's defiled,
And tainted, learns to look.

Bejan Matur

I've Learnt, It Hurts To Be In This World

All the crimson stones on earth
Are smeared with god's blood.
And so it is these crimson stones
Instruct us in our youth.
God, beside us
In our childhood,
Touches our earrings,
Our necklaces too;
Enters our shoes, the folds
Of our girlish ribbons
And hides.

I should buy a crimson dress and bed,
A crimson ring
And lamp.
That time must come
When motherhood begins, then ends.

Blood that knows to wait
Knows also to be stone.
I've learnt, it hurts to be in this world.

Crimson dark
Blue dark
And the beginning
Must surely make sense, -
Neither god nor our mothers desert us.

Every Woman Knows Her Own Tree

When I came to you
I meant to unfurl my wings
Over that lifeless city
Built of black stone,
To perch on the branch of a tree I found
And call out in pain.

Every woman knows her own tree.

That night I flew.
I passed the city where darkness was afraid to go.
When shadowless, the soul was alone. I howled.

Silent House

Silent house waiting in its courtyard,
Thought night was death. And left the world.

Child Graves

So we died.
Slid from darkness.
Beech trees saw,
Pebbles too.

Night and stars passed over us.
We were buried by the roadside.

Didem Madak was born in Izmir in 1970. She graduated from Dokuz Eylül University, Faculty of Law. In 2000 she won the İnkılâp Bookstore Poetry Prize for her first book of poems, *Grapon Kâğıtları*. She died in 2011.

Mr Parkinson

Each day crumbs of far-off nations fall
From the sun's pockets
Of a father of a poor family, a whiff
Of melancholy and sesame seeds.
As if a star like greta garbo has died
And the ironmongers walk their dark visions
In the street till sunset, and in every crack
And crevice of night the drunks puke up their day.
Sun is tucked away in a tax-return envelope.
Cheap clothes ripple on their hangers
Like a sea of bargains.

In the humid damp of morning, licking
And preening their fur, street cats in corners.
They gaze at the slanting rain,
Mangey cats of every colour.
Doughnut sellers, their greasy hands, greasy
Eyes, greasy hearted mangey men.
Seagulls uncertain of their claim
Descend on the markets of Kemeraltı.
Love and tears from thirty-three
Knife wounds dripping from their eyes.
And beneath the tower, there's Mr. Parkinson,
Each day at noon.
A man of this city
Waiting for an earthquake, each day at noon.

I Want to Write Poems With Flowers, Sir!

"Once I'm the Black Princess,
Only then will my life begin."
Pippi Longstocking

You're angry that I write poems with flowers, Sir,
But you don't know. I hide my bruised
And battered body behind flowery curtains.
I'm sitting in the dark. The lights are off.
The alarm clock rings until the spring winds out
And I bring back to mind a painful love affair.
This, like the irrelevant glint of a knife.
I'm an illicit rain, hiding in the clouds for years.
If I were to rain, I'd be worth my weight in gold.

I'm a cellar rat, Sir.
In my cellar only loneliness is king.
These days I'm as unbreakable as a plastic vase.
But I'm afraid. Soon enough
You'll be stepping on children playing in the park
With your size forty-three shoes
Which can't be good, Sir!

"It's dark already!" I say.
I toss breadcrumbs to birds
They peck at fragments of glass
In my dream in a bowlful of water
Colourful jigsaw pieces
—I want to tell you but you're not interested.
No, I don't think I can wait till morning
I really don't
People should tell their dreams straight away.
Sir, my soul was fourteen years old,
Aged in the coolness of a marble table.
To my soul they attached thin white artificial legs
I roamed the city with a squeak and creak.
They whistled even at my artificial legs.
And then laid siege to defenseless
Lines of flowers inside me
While "Groans of Orgasm" played at the cinemas.

I tried to escape. I couldn't.
That's why I find writing poems with flowers
Good for my soul, Sir.
So, there you are
I never forget a film.
I've often bunkered down in endless nights of cinemas.
I cried my heart out watching "Sophie's Choice."
If only they'd make a film of the kissing Guramis.
I'd have remembered it, for sure.
Can anyone forget the sound of a spinning wheel within them?

I'm used to remembering anyway.
Sir, I'm a "hoarder of things".

And now those giant ships are no more, Sir.
Those giant sails too
Now I have an urge to burn giant sheets of paper.
A while ago a cormorant dived beneath the waves
And hasn't surfaced yet.
If only it would reappear having swallowed the world
Death is such a big word isn't it, Sir?
I know I smell as bitterly as marigolds.
But do you know the beauty of a poor lover
Who cooks his sausage and eggs on a stove?
A rose, if it could see, would say to another
But, I'm lying of course
These days roses don't talk at all, Sir.

Zeynep Köylü

Zeynep Köylü was born in 1978. She won the Arkadaş Z. Özger Prize in 1997.

Life Inside

> *- for a woman I saw through her window*
> *while she was drying her laundry –*

mother, does laundry dry inside?
wind doesn't blow
every day it stabs the sky from its womb
I don't yearn for birds as I did
as if there's something wrong
that multiplies as I decrease

I've grown so used to the walls
I'd never have guessed I'd love them

as much as I love you
people get so used to things, I sew in the dark
I sew with darkness the unstitched
parts of night

mother, I heard a word called "life"
the other day, what does it mean?
I shelter behind a clove tree leaf
every second it stabs the sky from your womb
I forgot:
is that the voice in my mouth?

if sky could even fit in tiny rooms
mother, could a kite fly inside?

Sparrows Used to Bury the Moon

sparrows used to bury the moon
I used to plant a rose in time's ash
my stepmother would say "it won't grow"
my sky dirtied her white slip
I reeked of loneliness
and birds would be scared too

I came late to spring tranquillity
I'd sanctify the suicide of joys
a moonless gypsy would steal the night
glass was broken, light took fright
I'd kiss the water's wet mouth

I'd snap the branch where your dreams perch
the imperceptible figure of death would appear
my swarthy fingers
my face was there too

sparrows used to bury the moon
my stepmother would never see
how the rose began to bud

I Loved Impulsively

I left my dark waters long ago
don't excuse me

I spent my last night
                    with a young boy
who taught me the song of rain
the bare glimmer of rock

I held on to worn out stars
heedless of my errors
nights are a lover's liberation

I called out to no one
                    with no signs to hand
this mass of walls occluded
the dreams I affixed to spider's webs

I set my identity free with a traveler
left my voice in the silent mouths of the dead

my sorrows were
          glass-green
my sufferings chartless

in fleeting visions
                    my face's final season

I loved impulsively, don't excuse me

Gonca Özmen

Gonca Özmen was born in Burdur in 1982. Her two books, *Kuytumda* (2000) and *Belki Sessiz* (2008) have won several major awards. A selection of her poems in English, *The Sea Within* (2011), is published by Shearsman Books. She lives in Istanbul.

Partitions

I

I possessed a flaw
This ancient word is mine I said

For whomever doors open
I said for me they're closed

They formed me from consolation
Maybe carved me out of woe

Thus I felt the patience possessed of tongue
The voice too passing swiftly through evening

Gonca Özmen

II

Night's never-silent mouth stills now
Darkness inclines me towards the word

To dream you with those ancient lips
Your neck's garden with these dead lips

Beneath the flesh a soundless weariness
Leaves falling through a child's day-dreams

Where the sea has yet to end
Where everything narrows and broadens out

III

Let water's day-dream stay where it is
I'll offer myself to the leaf

The word I wilted will somehow return
I will bring to mind a blossoming flower

I will believe whatever night brings
For belief springs from our child-like side

With a child's mind I'll stroll around your words

IV

Then everything ends up in loneliness
A few chairs are enough to host grief

In evenings, the weariness I bring home says nothing of me
Unceasingly I caress the feathers of night

Flowers peer into vast emptiness
Wherever I go, it's into paleness

Butterflies dying on my face

Silent Perhaps

The forest prepares for night
Slowly strips its foliage

A bird's cloud-entangled dream

The wind speaks again of rocks
Wind tells of places it has seen

I say perhaps words will flow this time
Skin's desire release with rain

Maybe death and azans will baffle time
Somehow a child's severed arm blooms

O world, you shrink to nothing inside us

The sediment of words builds up
                at the bottom of a lake

Ceaselessly everything loses its voice

Blemish

I

The valley opened its secret to me
On a vast plain I found you
When the leaf dropped and the fig fell silent

There was a scorched side to me
And I placed you there

Take those sweet waters, those heady scents
A woman pours a river into herself
And what was far comes nearer still

Stay on the other side of touch
Embrace the absence you take me for

— Wind that blows through us
                is picking up leaves somehow

II

I thought everything stops with you
Time tells its secret to screens
A path winds through my body

I was those unending words
The pensive wood

I knew heavens descend with you
A squirrel zips into your lap

Takes me, leads me to a blemish
So I thought

You were those tireless waters
Those living sounds

I filled you ceaselessly

III

You started, so let everything pass
Let the geranium open in me, the sea recede

Let me have a dream with a seed inside
Let rivers pass through me, wild figs

Because morning has hurrying lips
There are sanctuaries! Darkness

If time stops let's put on silence
Let the light of your eyes know no return

Let the body's ache unwind in words
Let my face not fade in photographs

You began, so let everything pass
Quiet, said the ant, let time march on

Saliha Paker

Saliha Paker is Professor of Translation Studies and Head of the Department of Translation and Interpreting at Boğaziçi University, Istanbul. Since 1992, she has been an Honorary Research Fellow at the Centre for Byzantine, Ottoman and Modern Greek Studies, University of Birmingham. Her work in English includes an edited volume, *Translations: (re)shaping of literature and culture* (2002), various essays in international publications and translations of modern Turkish poetry and fiction, such as *Berji Kristin Tales from the Garbage Hills* (with Ruth Christie; 1993, 1996) and *Dear Shameless Death* (with Mel Kenne; 2001), both published by Marion Boyars.

George Messo

George Messo is a poet, translator, and editor. His books include *From the Pine Observatory* (2000), *Entrances* (2006), *Hearing Still* (2009) and *Violades & Appledown* (2012). He was shortlisted for the Popescu European Poetry Translation Prize in 2007 and in 2011. He holds degrees in Philosophy from the universities of Hull and Edinburgh, and a doctorate in Literary Translation from the University of East Anglia. He lives on a remote farm in northern Sweden with his wife and children, close to the town of Arjeplog.